QUESTIONED DOCUMENT EXAMINATION

Laboratory principles and practices

Ms. Labhini Rahangdale

Assistant Professor
Division of Criminology and Forensic Sciences
Karunya Institute of Technology and Sciences (deemed to be university)
Coimbatore - 641 114.
Tamilnadu, India.

Dr. Raju Nandhakumar

Professor
Division of Physical Sciences
Karunya Institute of Technology and Sciences (deemed to be university)
Coimbatore - 641 114.
Tamilnadu, India.

Made with ♥ on the Notion Press Platform

www.notionpress.com

Contents

Preface

Questioned Document Examination involves the meticulous analysis of various types of documents, including handwritten notes, printed texts, signatures, and photocopies. The goal is to uncover the truth behind their origins and authenticity. This book is designed to provide students with the knowledge, skills, and methodologies necessary to excel in this specialized "Questioned Document" area of forensic science. In today's digital age, where documents can be easily manipulated, the role of a forensic document examiner is more important than ever. The ability to scrutinize documents for authenticity, detect forgeries, and trace the origins of a document is a powerful tool in both criminal and civil investigations. This book is structured to offer a comprehensive, hands-on learning experience, enabling students to gain a deep understanding of the techniques and principles of questioned document examination.

In recent years, there has been a significant increase in the number of cases related to the examination and identification of photocopied documents. This rise can be attributed to the widespread use of photocopiers in daily life. The availability of advanced and sophisticated equipment, such as all-in-one machines, has made it easier for criminals to produce counterfeit or forged documents. They can manipulate or alter original documents using methods like scanning, cutting, and pasting to suit their own desires. Examining photocopied signatures and handwriting to determine the authorship of a document is no easy task in such circumstances. Criminals frequently utilize photocopiers to create fraudulent documents and make alterations to genuine ones. The field of forensic document examination plays a crucial role in forensic science, serving as a vital tool in the pursuit of justice. The exercises outlined in this book cover a wide range of topics, including handwriting analysis, ink analysis, and paper examination.

From the Authors

Welcome to the fascinating world of Questioned Document Examination (QDE), a crucial field of forensic science that uncovers the truth behind suspicious documents. We are excited to share our knowledge with you. QDE involves the scientific analysis of documents to detect forgeries and alterations, Identify the source of a document, Determine the age of a document, and reveal hidden or erased information. In many cases of forgery, it is crucial to determine the individual responsible for writing the document. This requires a thorough understanding of handwriting characteristics. This questioned document book has been specifically designed for the examination of various types of documents. Through this book, we aim to provide a comprehensive guide to QDE, covering its principles, techniques, and applications. A must-read for anyone involved in forensic document examination, this book provides a thorough understanding of the latest techniques and technologies. Furthermore, it offers comprehensive solutions for document examination, offering valuable insights and techniques for identifying forged documents. Whether you are a student, researcher, or practicing forensic scientist, we hope this book will inspire and equip you to tackle the challenges of document examination.

Format of the Lab Report

Lab reports should be prepared by hand. It should include tables and illustrations wherever necessary. Typically, a lab report should contain the following sections: title page, introduction, experimental section, results and discussion, conclusion, references and if possible a case study.

Safety Rules:

The laboratory is not a dangerous place to work as long as all necessary precautions are taken seriously. In the following paragraphs, those important precautions are described. Everyone who works and performs experiments in a laboratory must always follow these safety rules.

Gloves and Headgear: Crime scene investigation process includes analysis of samples and many rigorous activities. It is important to wear gloves/ lab coat and headgear etc.

Eating and Drinking: Any type of food is always prohibited in the laboratory. Smoking is not allowed. Anyone who refuses to do so will be forced to leave the laboratory.

Clothing and Footwear: Everyone must wear a lab coat during the lab and no shorts and sandals are allowed. Long hair should be securely tied back to avoid the risk of setting it on fire. If large amounts of chemicals are spilled on your body, immediately remove the contaminated clothing, and use the safety shower if available. Make sure to inform your instructor about the problem. Do not leave your coats and backpacks on the bench. No headphones and Walkman are allowed in the lab because they interfere with your ability to hear what is going on in the lab.

Fire: In case of fire or an accident, inform your instructor at once. Note the location of fire extinguishers and, if available, safety showers and safety blankets as soon as you enter the laboratory so that you may use them if needed. Never perform an unauthorized experiment in the laboratory. Never assume that it is not necessary to inform your instructor for small accidents. Notify him/her no matter how slight it is.

Laboratory Care and Waste Disposal: Remember that the equipment you use in this laboratory will be used by many other students. Please leave the equipment and all workspaces as you wish to find them. After the end of each lab, clean off your work area. Wash your glassware. When weighing any material on the balances, do not weigh directly onto the balance pan. Weigh your material on a piece of weighing paper. The balances are very sensitive instruments and should be treated with great care.

If you take more reagents than you need, do not put excess back into the bottle. It may be contaminated. Treat it as waste and dispose of it accordingly. It is most likely that, during any experiment you will perform, you will generate some waste chemicals and solutions to dispose of. Never put them down the sink unless specifically told to do so by your instructor. There will be inorganic, organic, and solid waste containers in the lab. Dispose of your waste in the appropriate container.

1

Understanding the Fundamentals of Handwriting

Aim:

To understand the fundamentals of handwriting by analyzing and comparing various handwriting samples.

Theory:

Understanding the class and individual characteristics of handwriting is essential for forensic document examiners. By analyzing the unique features of handwriting, experts can determine the authorship of a document and provide valuable evidence in legal proceedings. This process involves examining factors such as letter formation, spacing, slant, and pressure to identify patterns and distinguish between different writers. By honing their skills in handwriting analysis, forensic document examiners can make significant contributions to the field of forensic science. Before embarking on any experiments, it is crucial to have a thorough understanding of the characteristics of handwriting. This knowledge will enable us to effectively analyze various types of handwriting.

Requirements:

Handwriting samples, pencil and ruler.

Procedure:

In forensic handwriting analysis, there are twelve characteristics to be considered when analyzing a handwriting match.

- ***Line Quality*** is the thickness, strength, and flow of the letters. Some factors are if the letters are flowing, shaky, or very thick.
- ***Letter Spacing*** is the amount of space put between letters. The letters could all be connected or spaced drastically.

- ***Height, Width, and Size*** of the Letters is very self-explanatory; this simply analyzes the proportions of the handwriting. Is one letter unusually tall or short?
- ***Pen Lifts and Separations*** is the way the person writes. Do they stop before writing a new letter, or do they connect the letters? People usually use the same pen lifts, and so a forgery may stand out if all the letters are separated when the real signature connects them.
- ***Connecting Strokes*** is like pen lifts and separations. This analyzes whether the capital letters are connected to lowercase letters and if words are connected.
- ***Beginning and Ending Strokes*** looks at how the writer begins and ends their words. Do they end with a curl, and on an upstroke or a downstroke?
- ***Unusual Letter Formation*** takes note of any peculiar, unique capital or lowercase letters. Does the writer add any extra curls or loops where the average author would not?
- ***Shading (Pen Pressure)*** analyzes where the writer presses their writing utensil down the most, either on the upstroke or the downstroke. Where the most pressure is applied is where the script is thickest.
- ***Slant*** looks at which way the letters tend to slant, either to the left, right, or no slant at all. The most average slant is to the right. Baseline Habits is where the writer tends to write. It could be above the line, below the line, or on the line.
- ***Flourishments and Embellishments*** are large loops and swirls in handwriting. The most common flourishment is on letters such as lowercase "G", "J", and "F" - anything that involves a loop!
- ***Diacritic Placement*** is the way the author crosses their t's and dots their j's and i's
- ***Pen Pressure; weighty/solid pressure*** shows taking the angle harshly and showing devotion, but an extreme programming of strain proposes a short reaction to what gets apparent as a complaint even without the point of doing as such. They respond first and inquire questions later. Light pressure shows affectability to environment

and sympathy to other people anyway likewise can propose loss of force or equity

Please refer to the image below (Table 1 and Table 2) for a clearer understanding.

ANALYTICAL THINKING v-wedges for m, n-bottom baseline intersections	*sorts and separates information in assessing their value, evaluates information and supporting patterns*	
BLUNT increasingly heavy downward and forward middle final	*brings matters to a conclusion and thrusts it upon others*	
CONCENTRATION small writing	*focuses attention on one activity ignoring all other influences*	
CULTURAL REFINEMENT middle letter is printed with a capital letter	integration and discrimination of creative artistic and structural systems into one's mode of living	

Table 1

ELEMENTS OF HANDWRITING	PICTORIAL REPRESENTATION	TRAIT
t-bars		goal orientation, enthusiasm level etc
i-dots		ability to pay attention
loops		Upper loops-capacity for abstract thought, creativity ,imagination&selectivity in friendship.
Hooks		Initial hooks -Desire to acquire things. Final hooks – tenacity.
Pressure	Save Save	energy level, response to surrounding and stress level
Retracing		Repressed thoughts, feeling or emotions.
Wedges present		good at research &enjoy searching for answers.
End strokes	like had	Social attitude, real nature.
Zones		Upper zone-intellectual or abstract. Middle zone -daily action or tangible. Lower zone - desire, drives or biological.

Table 2

Observation Table:

Handwriting sample	Handwriting Characteristics	Explanation
	Slant	Right/Left?
	Size	Big, small or moderate?
	Formation of letter etc.	loop formation

Conclusion:

Through the analysis of handwriting characteristics, it is possible to

- Identify individual handwriting styles
- Determine the authorship of disputed handwriting samples
- Understand and interpret various experiments related to questioned documents

Viva Questions:

1. Define Handwriting.
2. Define line quality, slant and pen pressure.
3. What are the primary characteristics analyzed in handwriting to establish identity in forensic investigations?
4. How does a forensic document examiner differentiate between genuine handwriting and a forgery?
5. What role does line quality play in the forensic analysis of handwriting?
6. How do slant, pressure, and spacing contribute to the identification of handwriting?
7. What is the significance of connecting strokes in handwriting analysis?
8. How are individual letter formations used to distinguish between different handwriting samples?
9. What methods are used to analyze disguised handwriting in forensic investigations?
10. How does the analysis of handwriting involve both class and individual characteristics?
11. In what ways can handwriting be influenced by external factors such as physical condition or emotional state?
12. How is handwriting analysis used to detect alterations, such as erasures or additions, in a document?

13. What are some challenges in handwriting analysis, particularly when dealing with small samples or poor-quality documents?
14. How do forensic experts determine whether handwriting is the result of natural variation or intentional modification?
15. What technological advancements have enhanced the accuracy and reliability of forensic handwriting analysis?

Case Studies:

2

Identification of Class Characteristics in Handwriting

Aim:

To identify the class characteristics of handwriting samples.

Theory:

Handwriting, while inherently personal and unique to each individual, is also influenced by certain shared traits known as class characteristics. These characteristics are the result of common learning methods, cultural influences, and standardized writing systems. In forensic document examination, class characteristics play a crucial role in the initial assessment of handwriting samples, helping to categorize and compare handwriting across a group of individuals before focusing on individual traits. Class characteristics in handwriting refer to the general features shared by a group of writers. These characteristics are typically the result of common educational backgrounds, such as the way handwriting is taught in schools, and cultural norms. Class characteristics include aspects of handwriting like letter shapes, slant, spacing, and line quality that are consistent across a group of people who learned to write in a similar way.

Requirement:

Plain paper, pen, pencil, ruler etc.

Factors Contributing to Class Characteristics

1. **Educational Systems:**

   The way handwriting is taught in schools greatly influences class characteristics. For example, the Palmer Method and the Zaner-Bloser method are well-known handwriting instruction systems in the United States, each with distinct letter shapes and stroke sequences. Students trained in the same method tend to exhibit similar handwriting features.

2. **Cultural and Linguistic Influences:**

   Cultural factors, including the language and script used, influence handwriting class characteristics. For example, individuals who write in Roman, Cyrillic, or Arabic scripts will display different class characteristics based on the specific writing system. Cultural norms about handwriting style and the use of certain flourishes or decorations also contribute to class characteristics.

3. **Writing Instruments and Mediums:**

   The type of writing instrument and medium commonly used within a group can also create class characteristics. For instance, a group accustomed to using fountain pens may have different line quality characteristics than those who primarily use ballpoint pens or pencils.

4. **Temporal and Regional Trends:**

   Handwriting styles can evolve over time and differ by region, creating class characteristics specific to a particular era or geographic location. For example, cursive handwriting styles popular in the 19th century differ significantly from those taught today, and regional differences may exist even within the same language group.

Examples of Class Characteristics

1. **Letter Formation:**

   Standardized methods of teaching writing result in similar letter shapes and structures. For example, the way the letter "A" is formed in a particular writing system might be consistent among a group of people educated in the same region and time period.

2. **Slant and Angle:**

   A group of individuals taught to write with a rightward slant or to keep their handwriting upright will share this characteristic. The slant of writing can be a clear indicator of a particular writing style or method taught.

3. **Spacing and Proportions:**

   Class characteristics often include the spacing between letters, words, and lines, as well as the relative size of letters. These aspects are typically uniform among those who learned to write in the same way.

4. **Line Quality and Pressure:**

   The consistency of line thickness and the amount of pressure applied during writing are influenced by the type of writing instrument commonly used and the writing habits promoted by a particular instructional method. For example, some writing methods emphasize light, flowing strokes, while others promote firmer pressure.

5. **Punctuation and Grammar Usage:**

   The way punctuation marks are used or formed, as well as common grammatical habits, can reflect class characteristics, especially if these elements were emphasized in a specific educational system.

Significance in Forensic Document Examination

Class characteristics are particularly useful in the early stages of forensic handwriting analysis. They help forensic examiners:

1. **Narrow Down Suspects:**

   By identifying class characteristics, forensic examiners can quickly determine if a questioned document shares general handwriting traits with a group of potential suspects. This can be useful in excluding or including large groups of individuals.

2. **Determine Origin:**

   Class characteristics can provide clues about the origin of a document, such as the region where it was likely written or the type of educational background the writer may have had. This information can be crucial in investigative contexts.

3. **Identify Forgeries:**

   When examining potential forgeries, class characteristics can reveal inconsistencies. A forger might replicate individual characteristics but fail to reproduce the correct class characteristics, leading to discrepancies in the overall handwriting style.

Limitations:

While class characteristics are useful for categorizing handwriting, they are not sufficient for identifying a specific individual. Many people share the same class characteristics, so forensic examiners must also analyze individual characteristics to make a definitive identification.

Procedure:

1. **Collect Samples:**

   Obtain handwriting samples from multiple individuals. Ensure the text is identical across samples

2. **Observe Letter Forms:**

   Examine the general shape and style of letters, focusing on size, slant, and form. Use a ruler to measure the average height and width of letters in each sample. Record any common patterns observed, such as loop formations in "l" or "e."

3. **Analyze Pen Pressure and Line Quality:**

   Assess the uniformity of pen pressure across different samples. Note variations in line quality, such as smoothness or hesitations.

4. **Measure Slant and Alignment:**

   Use a protractor to measure the angle of slant for each sample. Observe the alignment of text (baseline adherence) and note any similarities.

5. **Record Findings:**

   Summarize the observed class characteristics and provide examples for each category.

Observation Table:

Sr. No	Sample image	Class Characteristics explanation
1.	Here's an example of my normal handwriting. Notice how letters are connected in a way that has little to do with word length - as in "normal" - 1, 2, 3 letters are grouped.	**Slant and Alignment: Right/Left or** baseline adherence? etc.
2.		
3.		
4.		
5.		

Conclusion:

Class characteristics reflect the basic structure shared by a group of writers, which can help narrow down a pool of suspects in forensic investigations.

Viva Questions:

1. What are class characteristics in handwriting?
2. How do class characteristics differ from individual characteristics in handwriting analysis?
3. Can you give examples of some common class characteristics in handwriting?
4. Why are class characteristics important in the initial stages of forensic handwriting analysis?
5. How do educational systems influence class characteristics in handwriting?

6. What role do cultural and regional factors play in the development of class characteristics?
7. How can the slant and angle of writing be considered a class characteristic?
8. In what ways can line quality and pen pressure be classified as class characteristics?
9. How can class characteristics help narrow down a pool of suspects in a forensic investigation?
10. Can class characteristics be used to determine the geographical origin of a handwriting sample? If so, how?
11. Why might a forensic examiner focus on class characteristics when examining a potential forgery?
12. What are the limitations of relying solely on class characteristics for handwriting identification?
13. How do historical changes in handwriting instruction affect class characteristics over time?
14. Can two individuals with the same class characteristics have identical handwriting? Why or why not?
15. How might a forensic document examiner distinguish between class characteristics and intentional forgery or mimicry?

Case Studies:

3

Analyzing Handwriting for Individual Characteristics

Aim:

To identify and document individual characteristics unique to a writer.

Theory:

Handwriting is often referred to as "brain writing" because it is a physical manifestation of an individual's neurological and motor processes. Despite being taught a standard way to write, every person's handwriting eventually develops unique traits. These unique traits, known as individual characteristics, are critical in forensic document examination for identifying or excluding potential writers of a questioned document. Individual characteristics in handwriting refer to the unique, personal traits that distinguish one person's handwriting from another's. Unlike class characteristics, which are general features shared by a group of writers, individual characteristics are specific to a single writer. These characteristics are shaped by various factors, including a person's neuromuscular coordination, writing habits, personality, and even the writing instrument and surface used. Factors Contributing to Individual Characteristics

1. **Neuromuscular Coordination:**

   The fine motor skills that control hand movements are unique to each person. This includes the pressure applied on the writing surface, the speed of writing, and the fluidity of strokes. Even slight variations in muscle control can result in distinct handwriting features.

2. **Writing Habits:**

   Over time, individuals develop habits that become ingrained in their handwriting. These habits may include specific ways of forming letters, connecting strokes, or consistent mistakes, such as frequent misspellings or omitted letters. These habitual traits are often unconscious and difficult to change.

3. **Personality Traits:**

   Psychological factors, including temperament and mood, can influence handwriting. For example, an anxious person might have shaky or uneven strokes, while a confident person might display bold, firm writing. Although personality traits influence handwriting, they are not as reliable for identification as motor habits.

4. **Writing Instrument and Surface:**

   The type of pen, pencil, or marker used, along with the writing surface, can influence handwriting characteristics. However, even when these variables change, the underlying individual characteristics remain consistent enough for forensic comparison.

Examples of Individual Characteristics

1. **Letter Formation:**

   The unique way a person forms letters is one of the most telling individual characteristics. Variations may include the shape of loops, the height and width of letters, or the distinct way a letter is finished (e.g., the flourish at the end of a "y").

2. **Slant and Angle:**

   The slant of the writing, whether it leans left, right, or is upright, can vary greatly between individuals. The angle of certain letters or strokes can also be a distinguishing factor.

3. **Pen Pressure:**

   The amount of pressure applied during writing can create distinctive line quality, such as thicker or thinner lines. This pressure can vary within the same document, but consistent patterns can be identified as an individual characteristic.

4. **Spacing and Margins:**

   The spacing between letters, words, and lines, as well as the use of margins, can be unique to an individual. Some people may consistently write with wide spaces between words, while others might cluster their writing closely together.

5. **Baseline Alignment:**

   The alignment of handwriting relative to the baseline can be characteristic. Some individuals write with a steady, level baseline, while others may exhibit a rising or falling baseline throughout their writing.

6. **Connecting Strokes:**

   The manner in which a writer connects letters or lifts the pen between strokes can be a distinctive feature. Some writers may link letters in unusual ways, while others might consistently separate certain letter pairs.

7. **Flourishes and Embellishments:**

   Extra strokes, loops, or decorative elements added to letters or signatures are highly individualistic. These flourishes often reflect the writer's personality and are rarely found in exactly the same form in another person's handwriting.

Requirement:

Plain paper, pen, pencil, ruler etc.

Procedure:

1. **Collect a Known Sample:**
   - Obtain a handwriting sample from a known individual (exemplar).
   - Ensure that the content written matches a questioned document for comparison.
2. **Detailed Observation:**
   - Examine the handwriting for unique traits such as unusual letter formations, spacing, and connecting strokes between letters.
   - Use a magnifying glass or digital microscope to detect subtle features like ink skips, tremors, or pen lifts.
3. **Analyze Variations:**
   - Compare the known sample with the questioned document, focusing on specific letters or words.

- Identify and record any distinctive variations, such as the shape of the "t" crossbar or the curvature of "s."

4. **Overlay Technique:**
   - Place the questioned document and known sample on a lightbox or use transparent overlay sheets to compare alignment, spacing, and overall flow of handwriting.
   - Mark areas where the two samples diverge, indicating potential individual characteristics.

5. **Document Findings:**
   - Compile a list of individual characteristics and provide visual examples from the samples.

Observation Table:

Sr. No	Sample image	Individual Characteristics explanation
1.		Extra strokes, loops, or decorative elements added to letters or signatures are highly individualistic. These flourishes often reflect the writer's personality and are rarely found in exactly the same form in another person's handwriting etc.
2.		
3.		
4.		
5.		

Conclusion:

This exercise reinforces the importance of both class and individual characteristics in the forensic examination of handwriting.

Viva Questions:

1. What are individual characteristics in handwriting, and how do they differ from class characteristics?
2. Why are individual characteristics crucial for the identification of a specific writer?
3. Can you describe some common examples of individual characteristics in handwriting?
4. How do neuromuscular coordination and motor skills influence individual handwriting characteristics?
5. What techniques can be used to identify individual characteristics in a handwriting sample?
6. How does the analysis of individual characteristics aid in forensic document examination?
7. What role does pen pressure play in identifying individual characteristics in handwriting?
8. How can the shape and formation of specific letters be used to distinguish between different writers?
9. In a practical examination, how would you compare individual characteristics between a questioned document and a known sample?
10. How can baseline alignment be considered an individual characteristic in handwriting?
11. What are the challenges in identifying individual characteristics in a small or illegible handwriting sample?
12. How do connecting strokes between letters contribute to the identification of individual characteristics?
13. What tools and techniques are commonly used in a forensic lab to examine individual handwriting characteristics?

14. Can individual characteristics be consciously altered by the writer? If so, how might this affect a forensic analysis?
15. How does the use of a magnifying glass or digital microscope assist in identifying subtle individual characteristics?

Case Studies:

4

Simulated Forgery Detection in Signatures

Aim:

To detect simulated forgery in the given signature samples.

Theory:

Forgery may be defined as the creation of any false written document or alteration of a genuine one, with the intent to defraud. Forgery may consist of the filling up a blank on a document containinga genuine signature or materially altering or erasing instrument. The causal intent to swindle, grounded on knowledge of the wrong nature of the instrument, must complement the act. Modes of forgery may include bills of exchange, bills of lading, promissory notes, checks, bonds, receipts,order for money or goods, mortgages, discharges of mortgages, deeds, bonds, records, account books and certain kind of tickets or passes for transportation or events etc.

Types of Forgery:

To the subject of identification and comparison of signature and writing,forgeries may be classified as:

- Freehand, simulated or copied forgery
- Traced forgery
- Forgery by memory
- Forgery without model or forgery by impersonation

Simulated Forgery:

In the realm of forgery, individuals often attempt to replicate a model signature or writing style by mimicking the design of letters and other key features. The success of such endeavors hinges on the forger's skill, practice, and competency. While many forgeries turn out to be crude imitations, there are instances where a forger›s proficiency allows them to create a simulation that closely resembles the original, fooling those who only glance at the general outline of the letters without scrutinizing the finer details. Despite a forger's ability to mimic another individual's writing habits through extensive practice, it is nearly impossible to completely adopt every nuance of someone else's handwriting while simultaneously suppressing one's own unique writing style. This inherent challenge often leads to the failure of forgery attempts. Writing serves as a tangible reflection of the intricate interplay between mental processes and muscular movements that a writer has honed through years of practice. As handwriting becomes ingrained through repetition, it becomes a deeply ingrained habit that cannot be easily altered or replicated at will. This fundamental principle underscores the complexity of handwriting analysis and comparison.

Motives which incites the forger to simulate a genuine signature:

- Mainly to extort money illegally and it is this anticipation of gain and urges a person to do suchwrongful actions.
- Other options may be domestic or personal satisfaction.

Requirements:

Questioned and Standard signature specimen, magnifying glass.

Procedure:

1. The given questioned and admitted signature samples were compared for the detection of forgery. *{the questioned signature (the one that is alleged to have been forged) are examined. Then, it is compared to a collection of signatures that are known to be genuine. The genuine signatures are referred to as 'exemplars' or 'known signatures'.}*
2. The questioned signature is a sample currently under examination, being compared to an admitted signature. An admitted signature is the genuine signature obtained from individual documents such as a paycheque or a login register
3. Compare both the signature samples for identification of simulated forgery and authorship.

4. Different characteristics of both the signature samples were recorded in the observation table.

Signature Samples: (Stick here)

Observation Table:

Characteristics	Standard	Questioned
Initial and terminal strokes		
Pen lifts		
Tremor and hesitation marks		
Speed and pressure		
Skill		
Retracing		
Retouching		
Spacing between the letters		
Connection and strokes between letters		
Slant		
Shading		
The "I" dot		
"t" crossing		
Embellishment		

Result:

Based on the handwriting characteristics observed, both the requested and questionedspecimen signatures are from the same person/ from different persons.

Conclusion:

(Explain in detail the difference in characteristics of two samples and report).

Precautions:

- Treat all evidence submitted for document examinations in a way that protects the integrity of the evidence and minimizes the potential for contamination and deleterious change during handling, storage, and examinations.
- Do not mark anything with pen/pencil on the sample.
- Do not fold the document.
- Do not make any cuts on the document.
- Use magnifying glass for proper examination of the characteristics of the signatures.

Forensic Significance:

- Two signatures of a person cannot be same. If it is then, one of it might be traced or forged.
- This forms the basis of signature analysis in questioned documents.

Viva Questions:

1. What is forgery?
2. What are the different types of forgery?
3. What is forgery by memory?
4. What is the difference between simulated and traced forgery?
5. What the different characteristics of a forged signature?

6. What is simulated forgery, and how does it differ from other types of forgery?
7. What are the common techniques used by forgers to create simulated handwriting?
8. How do forensic experts identify simulated forgery in a handwriting sample?
9. What are the key signs or characteristics that indicate a handwriting sample may be a simulated forgery?
10. How does the examination of pen lifts and strokes help in detecting simulated forgery?
11. What role does the consistency of letter formations play in distinguishing genuine handwriting from simulated forgery?
12. How can the use of tracing or copying tools influence the detection of simulated forgery?
13. What challenges might a forensic document examiner face when analyzing a high-quality simulated forgery?
14. How do experts differentiate between natural handwriting variation and the deliberate inconsistencies found in simulated forgeries?
15. What methods or technologies are available to enhance the detection of simulated forgery in modern forensic science?

Case Studies:

5

Identifying Traced Forgery in Questioned Documents

Aim:

To detect traced forgery in the given questioned document sample.

Theory:

One form of forgery that is commonly used is tracing. Tracing involves a rather primitive method of replicating a signature or handwriting. Essentially, the forger obtains a genuine signature as a model, which can be held against a window, used with carbon paper or a light box, and then covered with another sheet of paper to trace over the original lines. Throughout this process, the forger makes various starts and stops, creating resting dots that are easily noticeable. Additionally, the forged writing tends to be slower and may result in indentations on the paper, which can be detected alongside the ink lines.

Forgery tracing is categorized based on the method of execution. Traced forgeries reveal the underlying rules present beneath the signatures. These rules may appear as indentations, carbon outlines, or ink strokes adhering to the rules. Direct tracing is a method in which the forger uses the original signature to trace onto forged documents without any assistance. On the other hand, when transmitted light is used beneath the document for tracing, it is classified as transmitted forgery. Another technique involves using carbon paper to create a carbon print of the original signature, which is then covered with ink using a pen. By utilizing tracing paper or butter paper, original signatures are traced through indentation and then filled in with ink using a pen to conceal the indented part on the document. These classifications of tracing forgeries provide insight into the execution style, which is crucial for understanding the nature of forgery. Familiarity with these methods of forgery is essential for identifying and distinguishing these forgeries.

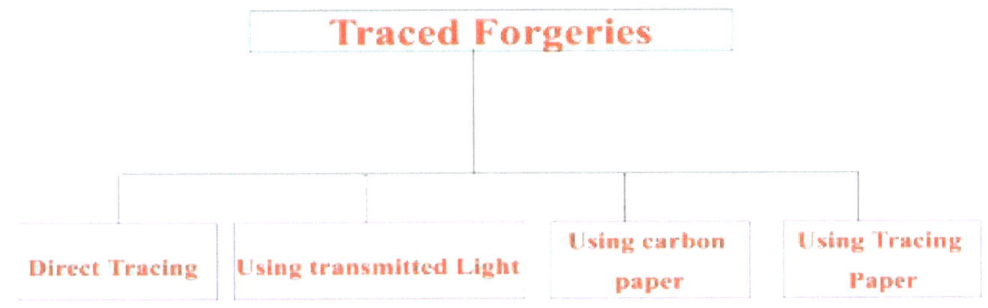

Classification of different types of tracing forgery

Requirement:

Questioned document, oblique light, magnifying glass and microscope.

Procedure:

When analyzing traced forgery, an examiner will carefully scrutinize any discrepancies between the forged signature or handwriting and the authentic, original signature or handwriting. By comparing various characteristics, the examiner can ascertain whether the traced forgery was executed by the same individual responsible for the original document. The key characteristics that are evaluated include: line quality, pen lifts and strokes, speed and rhythm, consistency, proportions and angles, distortions, and pressure. To begin the process of identifying a suspected forgery, the first step is to pinpoint the specific area of the document that is in question. This could involve scrutinizing a signature, a date, a handwriting sample, or any other element that raises doubts about the document's authenticity.

Next, it is crucial to thoroughly examine the original document to assess its legitimacy. This examination should include a close inspection of the paper, ink, and any other physical attributes that may provide clues as to whether the document is genuine or not. Finally, the suspected forged area should be subjected to a detailed analysis using a range of forensic techniques, such as microscopy, ultraviolet light, and infrared examination. These methods can help to uncover any inconsistencies or irregularities that may indicate tampering or forgery. It is essential to compare the handwriting or signature in question with known samples. Obtaining known samples of the suspected writer's handwriting or signature can be achieved by requesting a handwriting sample from the individual or examining other documents known to have been written or signed by the same person. After conducting a thorough examination and comparing the questioned document with known samples, a forensic document examiner can confidently form an opinion on whether the suspected area of the document is a forgery or not. This process is crucial in determining the authenticity of the document in question.

Analysis of a Traced Signature:

- The presence of pencil or carbon outlines alongside the signature suggests a tracing process has occurred.
- Indented outlines and strokes within the signature are evident.
- Multiple forged signatures displaying suspicious similarities or rubber stamp effects overlap in significant areas.
- Utilize a stereomicroscope to examine disturbed paper fibers.
- Employ ESDA to detect indentations.
- Pay attention to handwriting characteristics such as line quality, hesitations, and spacing.

In the examination of traced signatures, it is crucial to meticulously analyze various elements to determine the authenticity and potential forgery of the document. By utilizing specialized tools and techniques, forensic experts can uncover subtle details that may reveal the true nature of the signature in question.

Observation Table:

Genuine Signature	**Traced Signature**
Characteristics observed	Characteristics observed

e.g., The presence or absence of pencil or carbon outlines alongside the signature suggests a tracing process has occurred.	*e.g., The presence or absence of pencil or carbon outlines alongside the signature suggests a tracing process has occurred.*

Result:

After analyzing both the signature sample and conducting a thorough examination, we will draw a conclusion as to whether the signature is being forged through tracing. Report the findings.

Viva Questions:

1. What are some common techniques used in traced forgery?
2. What types of documents or items are most commonly forged using traced forgery?
3. How can law enforcement officials and forensic experts detect traced forgeries?
4. What are some of the legal consequences for individuals convicted of traced forgery?
5. How can individuals and organizations protect themselves from becoming victims of traced forgery?
6. How has technology impacted the practice of traced forgery, and what new challenges does it present for investigators and analysts?
7. Can you explain what traced forgery is and how it differs from other types of forgeries?
8. What are the key characteristics you would look for when identifying a traced forgery?

9. Describe the process of how a forensic document examiner might detect a traced forgery.
10. How does the use of different writing instruments affect the detection of traced forgeries?
11. What role does pen pressure play in distinguishing traced forgeries from genuine signatures?
12. Can you discuss the importance of line quality analysis in the identification of traced forgery?
13. How would you differentiate between a traced forgery and a naturally varying genuine signature?
14. In what scenarios might a traced forgery be more challenging to detect?
15. How can the presence of tremors or hesitations in a signature indicate a traced forgery
16. What modern technological advancements assist forensic experts in detecting traced forgery?

Case Studies:

6

Detecting Normal and Disguised Handwriting

Aim:

To identify normal and disguised handwriting.

Theory:

Disguised handwriting, as mentioned above, is any deliberate arrange to alter one's handwriting to escape recognition. An anonymous letter, blackmail tries, ransom notes, threats, and similar documents are created by writers who feel their altered handwriting cannot be linked to them. It is typically straightforward to ascertain that handwriting is disguised due to stiffness or artificial look that characterizes it, however often it may be most challenging to identify the author of disguised writing.

Disguised writing may be viewed as a special form of forgery, since writer deliberately tries to alter the genuine writing for the purpose of hiding the personal identification. The complexity arises during the process of examination and identification of general as well as individual writing characteristic features, in analyzing the range and extent of natural variation in disguised writing. In disguising the writing, the writer may believe that they have able to alter or change the entire characteristic feature of their writing. Numerous forensic experimental case works carried out by the author related with examination of signature and handwriting and explained herein. Most commonly, the disguizers wrote in a way that drastically changed the pictorial image of their writing. However the minute and conspicuous features were less likely to be disguised. Most common method of disguised was used by the disguizer: use of increased pen pressure throughout the writing content, alter letter forms, change punctuation and line spacing, wrote with notable tremor or erratic movements in an attempt to completely distort the writing or create an appearance of simulation. However during the examination of handwriting characteristic to characterizing it as disguised writing, it is must to justify it by overruling the fact of writing content examining the other reasons such as mental disorder, physical illness, intoxication and natural tremor occurring in writings. Apart from these factors, the expert should also focuses on examination of the fraudulent tremor related with disguised nature, opposite-hand writing, and attempt of tracing in handwriting etc.

A large number of disguised writing has been examined to understand the characteristic writing features in such writings. In order to study the method applied by the disguizer in writing such writings and examination of detailed features of disguised writings reveals various changes in writing features such as: lack of uniformity of letter size, inconsistency in writing contents, unnatural pen pressure including much more other features. On the basis of forensic examination of such features in detailed, for an expert, it is possible to understand the disguised nature of writing content. Examination of various extensive disguised writings reveals that most of the disguised nature of writing and signatures is done by mean of changing the characteristic feature of the writing content such as by alteration in base line of signature, slant, beginning and ending stroke, degradation in line quality, the exclusive use of non-cursive upper class letter such as B,D,R,P, blunt start, blunt end, changed form of letter formation either by eliminating curve stroke or During the examination of various handwriting contents related with disguised writings in routine case work, sometime the author encountered the difficulty in examination of finding significant handwriting characteristics features for fixing authorship. However due to consciousness during the act writing, by masking identity writer leave some point of their original hand characteristic feature which depend upon the skill of the writer gives also a very suitable identifying clue to fix the authorship.

Requirements:

Pen, scale, magnifying glass, A4 sheets, pencil etc.

Procedure:

- Collect/prepare Questioned and specimen sample.
- Questioned sample compared with specimen sample.
- Both the handwriting samples were examined for class and individual characteristics.

- To fix authorship we analyzed similarities/natural variation/ formation of each letters/overall structure of certain words in both the handwriting samples.
- We then specifically examined initial stroke i.e. similar nature of commencing stroke in execution of letters.

Observation Table:

FOR SAMPLE 1:

Sr. No	Questioned sample	Specimen Sample	Disguised in nature or not (YES/NO)	Reasons for yes/no
1.	Paste your sample here	Paste your sample here		*(Write individual and class characteristics)* 1. Initial and terminal strokes 2. Tremor and hesitation marks 3. Retouching, retracing etc. 4. Formation of letters etc

FOR SAMPLE 2:

Sr. No	Questioned sample	Specimen Sample	Disguised in nature or not (YES/NO)	Reasons for yes/no
1.	Paste your sample here	Paste your sample here		*(Write individual and class characteristics)* 1. Initial and terminal strokes 2.Tremor and hesitation marks 3.Retouching, retracing etc. **4.** Formation of letters etc

Result:

Among the given samples, the following are the disguised ones....

a.

b.

c.

Forensic Significance:

- Disguised writing is any deliberate attempt to alter one's handwriting to prevent recognition. Anonymous letters, blackmail attempts, ransom notes, threats, and similar documents arc created by writers who feel their altered handwriting cannot be attributed to them.
- We can identify ingenuity of handwriting and helps in individualization after analyzing disguised nature of writings.

Viva Questions:

1. What is disguised handwriting?
2. What are embellishments?
3. What is slant and alignment?
4. How will you examine disguised handwriting?
5. What are class and individual characteristics?
6. What is forensic significance of examining questioned documents?
7. What is disguised handwriting, and how can it affect the analysis of questioned documents?
8. What are the common methods individuals use to disguise their handwriting, and how can forensic experts detect these methods?
9. How do you differentiate between naturally varied handwriting and deliberately disguised handwriting?
10. What role do writing habits and characteristics play in identifying disguised handwriting?
11. Explain the importance of line quality and stroke formation in identifying disguised handwriting.

12. How can the use of non-dominant hand writing be identified as an attempt at disguise in handwriting analysis?
13. What techniques or tools are commonly used in the forensic analysis of disguised handwriting?
14. Can disguised handwriting be conclusively linked to an individual? If so, how?
15. Discuss a case study where disguised handwriting played a crucial role in the forensic analysis of a questioned document.

Case Studies:

7

Examining Erasures and Obliterations in Questioned Documents

Aim:

To examine obliterations and erasures in given question document.

Requirement:

Questioned document, oblique light, magnifying glass, microscope, erasure and blade etc.

Theory:

The Basic Questioned Document Examinations encompass a variety of tasks, including:

- Comparing signatures or handwriting
- Detecting any alterations, deletions, insertions, or substitutions in documents
- Deciphering erased or obliterated text
- Identifying counterfeit documents
- Analyzing charred, torn, water-soaked, or stained documents
- Conducting ink and paper analysis
- Age of documents
- Sequencing of entry made
- Examination of indented or accidental or secret writings
- Examination of matters written by machines like typewriters, photocopier or printer

These examinations are crucial in determining the authenticity and integrity of documents, and are essential in legal proceedings and investigations. By utilizing a combination of forensic techniques and expertise, our team is able to provide accurate and reliable results in a timely manner. Trust us to handle your questioned document examinations with professionalism and precision. The documents in question are suspected to have been tampered with through the removal, erasure, or addition of words, strokes, or lines. These alterations may have occurred in blank spaces, or by replacing or modifying existing content through deletion or addition of strokes or letters. Additionally, discrepancies may be identified based on the consecutive order of entries, consistency in pen and ink usage, changes in amounts, obliterations, sequence of writing, or typewriting on a folded paper to determine if the folding occurred before or after the writing.

Obliteration is the act of removing, destroying, or covering up evidence or information .Alteration is defined as any change to a document which gives it a different effect from that it originally possessed. If change is made after execution of a document and without the consent of the other party or concerned person, then such change is called fraudulent alteration.

- Addition in the document is defined as the insertion of any word, digit etc. which changes the meaning or value of the document. These insertions are made in such spaces as may have been left blank in the regular entries either in the middle or at the bottom of the page.
- The fraudulent overwriting to change the contents of documents are usually made in a careful manner and every effort is made by the preparator to conceal such changes made by him. When the original writing instrument and/ or ink are not available, the preparator tries to match the color of inks and nature of stroke. However, mostly he is not aware of the fact that the inks though of the same color are always not the same and they may differ considerably in their dye composition.
- Erasure is a method of alteration of any document. It may be a correction method made by erasing such as rubbing, scraping, or wiping out. Sometimes the term erasure refers to an effective revocation of a will or a portion of a will.
- Erasure is classified as: Chemical erasure, Physical erasure or Mechanical erasure.

- Physical erasure in a part of writing can be done by the abrasion of surface of paper with the help of rubber, sharp instrument such as razor blade, scalper, knife or Emory paper etc. The characteristic feature of physical erasure is removal of surface fibers of paper make the erased are comparatively thinner and translucent. But if some weak pencil writing is erased with a soft rubber erasure there is no mark of abrasion the surface fibers may not be damaged to the appreciable degree and those rubber particles get embedded in the fibers of paper. If sizing is damaged, the paper surface become porous and any subsequent writing over the erased area with fluid ink pen usually shows feathered ink lines. The application of sharp instrument causes disturbance on the surface finish of paper which can be detected by examining the document by oblique light i.e. by a beam of light falling at low angle. The soft rubber erasure particles can be detected under microscope or by subjecting the erased area to iodine vapor.

Procedure:

- Begin by carefully holding the suspected document and examining it in oblique lighting to detect any signs of alteration.
- Once an altered area is identified, encircle it for further examination.
- Utilize a microscope to closely observe the questioned document and analyze any alterations present.
- Employ a stereomicroscope for a more in-depth analysis, particularly for disturbances in paper fibers.
- Utilize UV light to reveal hidden or invisible characteristics of the document, such as watermark.

Observation Table:

Questioned Sample	Observations
	Erasures signs, any alteration, any addition of letter or removal of letters etc.

Result:

After examining a questioned document or sample for erasures or alterations, the following have occurred to the document:

a.

b.

c.

Viva Questions:

1. What are document alterations, and how do they differ from obliterations?
2. Explain the significance of document examination in forensic science.
3. What are the common reasons for alterations and obliterations in documents?
4. Describe the different methods used to detect alterations in documents.
5. How does infrared luminescence help in identifying alterations in documents?
6. What is the role of ultraviolet (UV) light in detecting obliterations?

7. Explain how Electrostatic Detection Devices (EDD) work in document examination.
8. How can chemical analysis be used to differentiate between inks in altered documents?
9. Can you describe a case where obliteration was detected successfully? What methods were used?
10. Give an example of how an alteration in a document might be identified without using advanced technology.
11. What are the challenges in presenting evidence of document alterations in court?
12. How do forensic document examiners ensure the integrity of the original document during examination?
13. What is the difference between mechanical erasure and chemical erasure, and how can each be detected?
14. How does the examination of handwriting help in identifying alterations or additions to a document?
15. What are the recent advancements in the field of document examination concerning alterations and obliterations?

Case Studies:

8

Printer Identification and Linkage Analysis

Aim:

To examine and identify the type of printer used and to establish a linkage of the questioned document with the alleged printer by analyzing different printed documents.

Theory:

Printed documents are very frequently encountered in forensic cases as disputed or questioned documents. With increasing number of such cases, the printer inspection in has become a major requirement in questioned document examination in recent years considering the extensive use printers in document creation in comparison to handwritten papers. Also, the counterfeiting of printed documents by various printers have been recorded at a large scale in last two decades. In such cases, it is very much required by the investigators to examine and identify the type of printer used and to establish a linkage of the questioned document with the alleged printer.

The examination, analysis and identification of various types of printed documents on the basis of their specific characteristics including resolution, edge contrast, letter roughness and feathering formed from diverse printers to differentiate and classify them for forensic questioned document examination and to assist the forensic expert and questioned document examiner thorough such investigations. Each printer has its uniqueness in printing documents, and this study aims to figure out that particular uniqueness at the documents after printing from the alleged printer. The observations revealed substantial differences in the letter's characteristics. This study may be a useful to discriminate the documents printed from different types of printers.

A. Working of Ink jet Printer

Ink jet printing is quite common and employs a swinging print head that **sprays** ink onto the paper as it travels through the carriage. It's used for printing on large scales, images that need more color fidelity (such as HD photos), and printing on certain special media. Any ink jet printer has three major elements i.e. the printer head, carriage, and advance mechanism. As the carriage swings back and forth in the direction of scan, the fixed print head fires ink onto paper.

B. Working of Laser Printer

Laser printers use electrostatic digital printing to generate high-quality tests and graphics, as well as moderate-quality images. Over a negatively charged cylinder known as the drum, a laser beam passes back and forth which the charged powdered ink from toner is selected and then collected electrically before transferring the image on to the paper, which is then printed The xerographic printing method is used by laser printers. The printing process begins with the work of a laser scanner, which forms an image and then generates a laser beam which is then directed through the glass interface to replicate the image underneath it. A mirror located in the printer then reflects this image, which is centered on a lens. The image is moved to the photocopier belt, where it is converted into printable form by a developer device. Laser printing, on the other hand, differs from analog photocopiers.

The image is created in a laser printer by scanning or imaging the medium directly across the photoreceptor of the printer. As a result, laser printing can copy and print images much faster than most printers and photocopiers.

Requirements:

Pen, scale, magnifying glass, A4 sheets, pencil etc.

Procedure:

- Two samples were collected from ink jet and laser printer.
- One sample collected from ink jet printer and one sample collected from laser printer.

- Both the sample have been analyzed for their specific characteristics including resolution, edge contrast, letter roughness and feathering formed from printers to differentiate and classify them for forensic questioned document examination.

Observations:

Comparison of the characteristic features of the printed documents by two types of printers

Comparison Parameters	Ink jet Printers	Laser Printers
Overall Print Quality (Resolution)		
Letter Contrast		
Edge Roughness		
Presence of spur marks		
Ink thickness in document		
Wear and tear marks		
Abnormal marks due to malfunctioning of printer		
Unique characters		
Inking uniformity		
Feathering of letters		

Examination of Printed Document

Feature Detection

1. **Degree of edge contrast** - Sharpness, smudging, waviness at the edges of letters.
2. **Degree of edge roughness** - The edges are sometimes uneven and on high magnification looks degraded.
3. **Spur marks (Tremorous Printing)** - Usually seen in inkjet printed document.

Result:

Examination of printed documents has been successfully studied and printer origin and printer identification has been established.

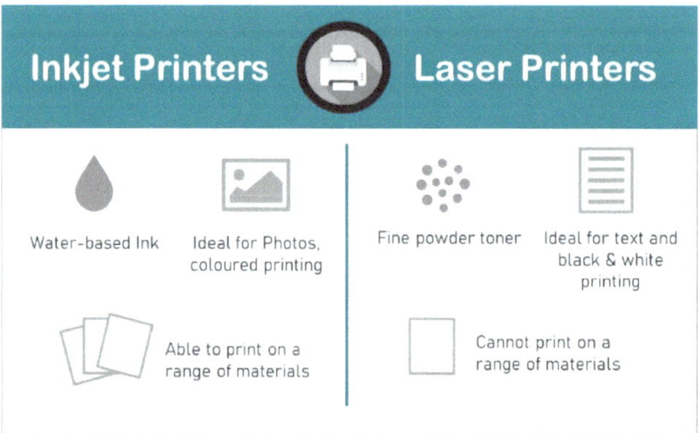

Viva Questions:

1. What is document?
2. What is questioned document?
3. Why we analyze printed documents?
4. Can we identify which printer is new one and old one? If yes then quote a reason?

5. What is edge roughness in printer?
6. What is the significance of printed document examination in forensic science?
7. Explain the differences between various types of printing technologies (e.g., inkjet, laser, offset) and their forensic relevance.
8. How can you differentiate between an original printed document and a photocopy?
9. Describe the methods used to identify the source printer of a document.
10. What role does the analysis of toner or ink composition play in printed document examination?
11. Can you explain a scenario where forensic examination of a printed document helped in solving a case? What techniques were used?
12. What challenges might arise when presenting evidence from printed document examination in court?
13. How do you ensure the authenticity and integrity of a printed document during forensic examination?
14. What is the significance of identifying printer defects or imperfections in forensic examination?
15. How can microscopic examination assist in the analysis of printed documents?

Case Studies:

9

Examining Photocopies for Alterations and Origin

Aim:

To examine photocopies of documents in order to identify possible alterations, determine the origin of the copies, and analyze any distinguishing features that could link the copy to a specific photocopy machine or original document.

Theory:

The examination of photocopies is a critical component of forensic document analysis. This process involves scrutinizing photocopied documents to establish their authenticity, detect any alterations, determine the specific copying machine used, and potentially trace the copy back to its original source. In recent years, there has been a notable uptick in cases necessitating the examination and identification of photocopied documents. This surge can be attributed to the widespread utilization of photocopiers in everyday life. The proliferation of advanced technology, including all-in-one machines, has facilitated the production of counterfeit or forged documents by individuals seeking to deceive others. These individuals may employ various techniques, such as scanning, cutting, and pasting, to manipulate original documents to suit their illicit purposes. In such scenarios, establishing the authorship of a document based on photocopied signatures or handwriting poses a formidable challenge. Criminals frequently exploit photocopiers to fabricate fraudulent documents, altering genuine content by inserting false information, removing authentic details, or substituting entire sections with counterfeit material to advance their criminal endeavors. This presents a significant obstacle for forensic document analysts tasked with scrutinizing these photocopied documents to address inquiries pertaining to criminal investigations.

Materials Required

Photocopies of questioned documents, original documents (if available), high-resolution scanner, digital microscope, magnifying glass, Forensic light source (e.g., UV, IR), calipers or a ruler, Electrostatic Detection Apparatus (ESDA), Comparison microscope, Toner particle analysis kit, Document Examiner's kit (scalpel, tweezers, etc.) and. Computer with image analysis software.

Procedure:

A. Visual Examination

To identify any visible discrepancies, alterations, or anomalies in the Photocopy.

Steps:

1. Place the photocopy on a clean, flat surface under adequate lighting.
2. Examine the document for signs of alterations, such as uneven toner application, smudging, or unusual margins.
3. Look for any missing or distorted characters, which may indicate tampering.
4. Compare the photocopy with the original document (if available) to note any differences in layout, font, or spacing.
5. Record observations in the provided observation table.

Observation Table for visual examination:

Sample	Discrepancies Noted	Toner Application	Alterations Observed	Comments

B. Microscopic Examination

To observe fine details and toner application under magnification.

Steps:

1. Use a digital microscope to examine the photocopy at varying magnifications.
2. Focus on areas where text or images appear distorted or irregular.
3. Look for toner distribution patterns, edge effects, and any anomalies that may indicate tampering or copying errors.
4. Compare the findings with known standards or original documents.
5. Record all observations in the observation table.

Observation Table for Microscopic Examination:

Sample	Toner distribution	Edge Effects	Anomalies Observed	Comments

C. Electrostatic Detection Apparatus (ESDA) Examination

To detect indented writing or impressions on the photocopy that may not be visible to the naked eye.

Steps:

1. Place the photocopy on the ESDA device.
2. Gently pass the ESDA film over the document.
3. Apply the charge to visualize any indented impressions.
4. Analyze the resulting patterns to determine if any underlying text or alterations are present.
5. Compare any detected impressions with the original document, if available.
6. Document the results in the observation table.

Observation Table for ESDA Examination:

Sample	Indented Writing detected(YES/NO)	Description of indentations	Comments

D. Image Analysis

To compare the photocopy with the original document using digital image analysis software.

Steps:

1. Scan the photocopy and the original document (if available) using a high-resolution scanner.
2. Use image analysis software to overlay the scanned images and compare them for discrepancies.
3. Analyze the alignment, spacing, and any signs of manipulation in the photocopy.
4. Look for digital artifacts that may indicate tampering.
5. Record the results of the analysis in the observation table.

Observation Table for Image analysis:

Sample	Alignment Discrepancies	Digital Discrepancies detected(YES/NO)	Comments

Results and Interpretation

Please provide a summary of the findings obtained from each examination technique. Compare the photocopy with the original document to identify any alterations or inconsistencies. Analyze the toner composition and microscopic details to potentially determine the specific photocopier used. Lastly, discuss the overall authenticity of the photocopy based on the evidence gathered.

Conclusion

After carefully observing and analyzing the photocopy, it is imperative to draw a conclusion regarding its authenticity. *(Determine whether the document has been tampered with or if it remains consistent with the original. Additionally, it is important to address any limitations encountered during the examination and recommend further analysis if deemed necessary.)*

Viva Questions:

1. What is the primary goal of examining photocopies in forensic document analysis?
2. What are some common signs of tampering or alterations in a photocopy?
3. How does toner application vary between different photocopy machines, and how can this be detected?
4. What role does microscopic examination play in analyzing xerox copies?
5. How can a digital microscope help in identifying issues in a xerox copy?
6. Describe the process of using an Electrostatic Detection Apparatus (ESDA) in photocopy examination. What types of evidence can it reveal?
7. Why is it important to compare the xerox copy with the original document, if available?
8. How can toner particle analysis be used to identify the type or brand of photocopy machine used?
9. What are the typical methods for detecting indented writing or impressions on a photocopy?
10. How can image analysis software be utilized in comparing xerox copies with original documents?
11. What are some potential limitations of photocopy examination in forensic analysis?
12. How does the resolution of the scanner affect the quality of the photocopy analysis?
13. Describe how you would use UV or IR light sources in the examination of photocopies. What are you looking for?
14. What factors might affect the accuracy of a photocopy, and how can these factors be assessed?

15. Discuss how different types of photocopy machines and their settings might impact the appearance of a photocopy. How can this information be useful in forensic investigations?

Case Studies:

10

Ink Analysis for Document Authentication

Aim:

To perform ink analysis on questioned documents to identify and compare ink characteristics, and to determine if alterations or forgeries have been made.

Theory:

Ink is a colored liquid used to create colored surfaces in various fields such as painting, text, or design. The origins of ink can be traced back to ancient Egypt, specifically the Old Kingdom. The ancient Egyptians utilized red pens and required ink for their writings. By 2697 BCE, the Egyptians had developed ink, deriving its black color from carbon black or finely pulverized pin ash. These components were mixed with lamp oil containing gelatin made from boiled donkey skin. However, the unpleasant smell of the ink led the Egyptians to add musk oil for a more pleasant aroma. During the same period, the Chinese were also experimenting with ink, using natural dyes mixed with graphite and water to create ink that could be applied with brushes. India ink was developed in India during the fourth century BCE, made from burned bones, tar, pitch, and other materials. Writing was accomplished using this ink and a sharp pointed needle. The history of ink reveals the ingenuity and creativity of ancient civilisations in developing materials for communication and artistic expression.

Ink analysis plays a crucial role in forensic document examination, enabling forensic scientists to accurately identify and compare inks present on questioned documents. This meticulous process aids in determining the presence of multiple inks, detecting any alterations made to a document, and establishing a potential match between the ink used and a suspect pen. The focus is on various techniques such as visual examination, microspectrophotometry, thin-layer chromatography (TLC), and infrared (IR) or ultraviolet (UV) examination. These techniques are essential in providing accurate and reliable results in the field of forensic document examination.

Materials Required

- Questioned document(s)
- Known ink samples (exemplars)
- Microscope
- Microspectrophotometer
- Thin-layer chromatography (TLC) plates
- Solvent system for TLC (e.g., ethanol, acetone, water)
- UV light source
- IR light source
- Scalpel or blade (for micro-sampling)
- Capillary tubes or micropipettes
- Ruler and protractor
- Gloves and protective eyewear
- Sample vials
- Digital camera or document scanner

Procedure:

A. Visual Examination:

1. To properly analyze the questioned document, it is essential to place it under a microscope and carefully examine the ink strokes.
2. Pay close attention to any variations in ink color, thickness, or application method, such as distinguishing between pen and printer ink.
3. If possible, compare these characteristics with known ink samples for further validation.
4. Be sure to meticulously document all observations in the provided observation table for thorough analysis.

B. Infrared and Ultraviolet Examination:

To detect any alterations in the document that may not be visible under normal light conditions.

To properly examine the document, follow these steps:

1. Position the document under both an infrared (IR) and ultraviolet (UV) light source.
2. Take note of any alterations in the ink's appearance, including fluorescence or absorption variances, when viewed under the UV light.
3. Utilize the IR light source to detect any ink that may be imperceptible to the naked eye.
4. Document your observations in the designated table.
5. By meticulously following these procedures, you will be able to thoroughly analyze the document and accurately record your findings.

C. Thin-Layer Chromatography (TLC):

To separate the components of the ink to identify its chemical composition

1. To conduct ink analysis, begin by delicately extracting a small ink sample from the document using a scalpel or blade.
2. Next, carefully apply the ink sample onto a TLC plate using a capillary tube. Then, prepare a solvent system in a developing chamber.
3. Place the TLC plate in the solvent and allow the solvent to ascend the plate, effectively separating the ink components.
4. Once the process is complete, remove the plate, allow it to dry, and observe the separation pattern.
5. Subsequently, compare the pattern to known ink samples or reference standards.
6. Finally, calculate the Retention Factor (Rf) values for each component to further analyze the ink composition.

Observation table:

Visual Examination:				
sample	Ink color	Ink density	Stroke of ink	Inference

IR/UV Examination:			
sample	UV Fluorescence (YES/NO)	IR Absorption	Inference

Thin-Layer Chromatography:				
sample	Rf (Component 1)	Rf (Component 2)	Rf (Component 3)	Inference

Results:

- Examine the data recorded in the observation tables to identify any similarities or differences among the ink samples.
- Assess whether the questioned document contains inks from multiple sources, which could suggest potential alterations.
- Utilize the TLC results to pinpoint the specific type or brand of ink, if feasible, by comparing Rf values with established standard.

Conclusion:

Please provide a summary of the findings obtained through the different analysis techniques. *(Determine whether the ink analysis corroborates the authenticity of the document or indicates potential forgery or alteration. Additionally, address any limitations that were encountered during the analysis and recommend further testing if deemed necessary.)*

Viva Questions:

1. What is the primary purpose of ink analysis in forensic document examination?

2. Can you explain the difference between visual examination and chemical analysis in ink analysis?
3. How does thin-layer chromatography (TLC) work in the context of ink analysis?
4. What is a Retention Factor (Rf) in TLC, and how is it calculated?
5. Why is it important to compare questioned ink samples with known ink standards during analysis?
6. What are some of the challenges in extracting ink samples from a document for analysis?
7. How can infrared (IR) and ultraviolet (UV) light be used to detect alterations in a document?
8. What are the advantages of using microspectrophotometry in ink analysis?
9. In what situations would you choose to use IR or UV light over other methods of ink analysis?
10. How can ink aging affect the results of ink analysis, and how can this be accounted for?
11. What role does the solvent system play in thin-layer chromatography for ink analysis?
12. Can different inks from the same manufacturer produce different results in ink analysis? If so, why?
13. How would you identify if multiple inks were used on the same document?
14. What precautions must be taken to avoid contamination of ink samples during analysis?
15. How do the results of ink analysis contribute to determining the authenticity of a document?

Case Studies:

11

To Perform Ink Analysis on Questioned Documents

Aim:

To analyze the dyes in ballpoint pen inks.

Theory:

Dyes are coloring materials that have an affinity to adhere to a solvent medium. Unlike other organic compounds, dyes are inherently colorful as they absorb light within the visible spectrum, ranging from 400 to 700 nm. They contain at least one chromophore, which is a color-bearing group with a conjugated system that exhibits resonance of electrons. These phenomena are responsible for the vibrant colors of the compound. Without any of these characteristics, the molecule would lack color. In addition to the chromophore, there are auxochromes, also known as color helpers, that contribute to the color of a compound. Common auxochromes include carboxylic acids, sulfonic acids, amino groups, and hydroxyl groups.

Organic colorants can be classified into two categories based on solubility: dyes and pigments. Dyes are soluble in water and organic solvents, while pigments are typically insoluble in both. Dyes can be used to color any substance, whereas pigments are primarily used to color polymeric substrates due to differences in their mechanisms. Pigments simply mix with the polymer before the formation of the article, without interacting with the substrate or altering its crystal structure.

Examination Of Ink Dye:

The documents which are alleged in case of forgery and alterations are frequently requiring the ink examination. And while doing so, the criminal forgery or generally not aware of the fact that the inks of similar colors are not always identical in their compositions and mere resemblance in the color of ink has little significance. Before starting the examination, always the non-destructive methods are used in examination of ink because it can preserve the original sample and that can be further analysis.

1. Physical Examination

This includes the optical examination of ink with the help of hand magnifier or compound microscope to determine:

- The type of ink used (ball point pen, fountain pen or fiber tip etc)
- Colour of ink
- Comparison of secondary colour shades, ultraviolet rays are used to compare the degree of fluorescence.
- Infrared rays are used to differentiate dyes and pigments and especially ball point pen inks.

2. Chemical examination

If two inks are found same from the physical examination then chemical examination can be avoided, because test results in the alteration of at least some part of the document.

The chemical analysis of ink can be conducted in two different ways

- Performing chemical spot tests on the punched out fragments of ink strokes or on the ink strokes itself.
- Chromatographic analysis for isolation and characterizing various dyestuff inks.

3.Thin layer chromatography (TLC):

Thin-layer chromatography (TLC) is considered to be the most suitable technique for isolating and identifying various components of inks. In these techniques a thin-layer plate is prepared by coating a glass plate with silica get or aluminum oxide but the readymade silica gel G plates are available in plate. Depending on the amount of ink deposited on the paper, 1 to 10 plugs of ink are removed with the help of a spatula or hypodermic needle and the ink is dissolved in the minimum quantity of a suitable solvents. A few micro liters of the solution are spotted with a capillary tube onto the layer on the thin-layer plate and plate is then placed in a closed jar having selected solvents in fixed ratios. The liquid slowly begins to rise up the plate and when it moves past the sample spot, the components of the sample get separated and get located at different heights. When the liquid phase has moved a sufficient distance the plate is removed from the jar and the Rf value of different spot are recorded.

For differentiation of two inks, their spots are marked on the same TLC plate and if these samples show same number of spots with the same Rf values and colors, then the two inks are identical in their dyes composition otherwise not.

Rf value is defined as the distance traveled by the component divided by the distance traveled by the liquid moving phase.

Different solvent systems for ink analysis:

- Butanol: ethanol: water - 50:15:10
- Ethyl acetate: cyclohexane: methanol: ammonia - 70:15:10:5
- Ethyl acetate: butanol: ammonia - 50:35:5
- Ethyl acetate: ethanol: water - 70:35:30
- Toluene: acetate: ethanol: water - 30:60:7:2

Requirement:

Capillary tubes, TLC plates, cavity plates, beakers, watch glass, ethyl acetate, methanol and water.

Procedure:

Punch out a small sample from the suspected document. Extract the ink in cavity plate by using acetone. Give spot of the sample on TLC plate. Prepare solvent system in the beaker by using ethyl acetate, ethanol and distilled water in the ratio of 7:3:2. Run the TLC and calculate Rf value for each spot.

Observation table:

Sample	Color of ink	No. of spots	Color of spots	Rf value of spots
A		3		
B				
C				

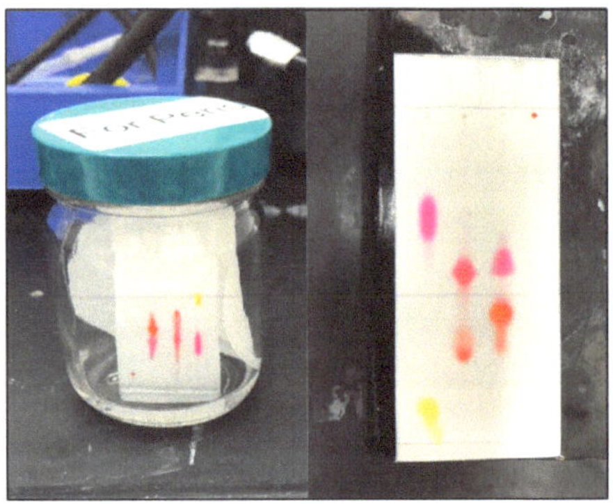

Result:

Ink analysis by using thin-layer chromatography was performed for three different ink samples and the Rf values were found to be as follows:

Sample A:

Sample B:

Sample C:

Viva Questions:

1. What is the principle for TLC?
2. What are the other methods used for ink analysis?
3. What is the forensic significance of ink analysis?

4. What are the key components of ballpoint pen ink, and why are they important in forensic analysis?
5. How does the aging of ink affect forensic analysis, and what methods are used to estimate the age of the ink?
6. What is the significance of analyzing the chemical composition of ink in forensic document examination?
7. How can ink analysis help in determining the authenticity of a document?
8. What are some common challenges faced in the forensic analysis of ballpoint pen ink?
9. Can you explain the difference between ballpoint pen inks and other types of writing inks in forensic analysis?
10. What is Thin Layer Chromatography (TLC), and how is it applied in forensic ink analysis?
11. How does TLC help in distinguishing between different inks used in a questioned document?
12. What are the limitations of using TLC in forensic ink analysis?
13. How do you interpret the results obtained from a TLC analysis in forensic document examination?
14. What role does the solvent system play in the TLC process, and how is it selected for ink analysis?
15. How can TLC be used in combination with other forensic techniques to enhance the analysis of inks?

Case Studies:

12

Identification of Different Writing Instrument

Aim:

Identification of different writing instrument.

Theory:

The choice of writing instrument is a crucial aspect of writing, as it can impact the way in which a person writes. For example, someone who is accustomed to using an ink pen may write differently than someone using a ballpoint pen, even though the difference may not be immediately noticeable. Writing instruments can be classified into various categories, such as paper, leaves, metals, pens, pencils, inks, plant juices, and chemicals. Historically, documents were prepared by writing on materials like bark from trees (such as papyrus) and metals like copper (tampatra). As human civilisation progressed, paper made from plants became the preferred writing surface. Different types of paper are now available for various writing needs. Before the development of modern writing instruments like pens and pencils, graphite and coal were commonly used.

The invention of pens led to the need for ink, which was initially derived from plant extracts or chemicals. In some cases, writing instruments like paint and plant juices have been used to convey messages, even at crime scenes. The choice of writing instrument can significantly impact the type of work being done and can be crucial for examiners in determining the source of writing. Personal habits also play a role in selecting a writing instrument, with some preferring gel point pens on smooth surfaces, while others opt for ballpoint pens on rougher surfaces. Ultimately, the selection of a writing instrument is a personal decision that can greatly influence the writing process.

Type of writing instrument and its specific characteristics:

Crayon:

A crayon is a type of writing instrument with a blunt tip that produces broad strokes when writing. Unlike pens or pencils, crayons do not have a sharp point for precise lines. They are solid in nature, containing wax or pigment, rather than liquid ink.

Ball Pen:

Characteristics of a ball pen

The ball pen consists of a small rotating ball fitted into a socket like device at the end of a tube which acts as the ink reservoir. The ink is fed through ball housing by the gravity and when ball rotates with the motion of pen, a thin film of ink in the form of the inked transforms on to the writing surface. The ink used in ball pen is a viscous past like material unlike usual fluid ink used in the fountain pen.

Identifying the work of a ball pen

This writing instrument has some different features which help in differentiating it from the other writing instruments. The features shown by the ball pen is given below:

- **Skipping**: In ball pen during writing sometimes the ink does not pass through the rolling ball and thus the production of strokes lacks ink in the strokes and produces an un-inked stroke. The skipping is shown below in the photograph in letter "L" of SUNIL.
- **Gooping:** Similarly, there is another term known as **gooping** which is known for the dark deposits of ink in the letters as shown in the letter "U" of SUNIL.

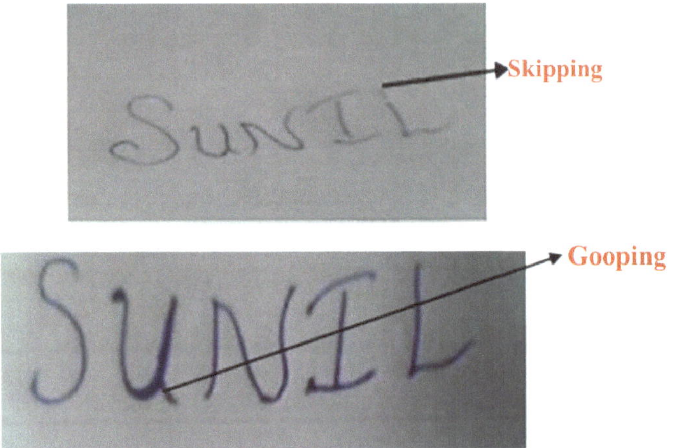

Porous tip pens:

The wider writing tips produces strokes with almost flat appearances which often has blunt beginning strokes and terminals. The inked line generally has smooth spreading of ink with smooth outlines of the margins of the strokes. The fine writing tips are generally made of porous plastic tips and these sometimes make grooves in the strokes, whereas the medium and wide writing points do not create any such indentation.

Roller Pens:

The ball pens so modified to write with fluid ink are commonly referred to as roller pens. These pens are like ball point pens in construction. These pens contain a water-based ink of the same general viscosity as found in fountain pen inks. The roller pens sometimes produce grooves in the strokes in the same manner as the ball pen and they sometimes show flowing back of ink in the ends of the strokes like the strokes found in the fountain pen writings. The ink from a roller pen is generally fairly broad with tapered beginning and ending strokes.

Pencil:

The pencil is one of the most ancient writing instruments and the best factor about this writing instrument is that it has maintained its place as an important writing instrument. This instrument has a non-flexible writing tip which is continuously rubbed off while depositing solid matter in the form of written line on the surface of paper. Depending upon the degree of hardness, writing pressure and nature of the writing surfaces, the pencil strokes vary in their nature and intensity. When one writes with a weak pressure the wear graphite is lesser and the deposits on the surface of paper is weak, producing lighter strokes and when one writes with heavy pressure the wear of graphite is more and the deposits on the surface of paper is greater producing darker strokes. Due to smooth and rounded point, the pencil, like a ball pen enables the writer to write faster than he would write with fountain pen. This can be of little benefit to all the forgers if the bank allows the signature on the withdrawal form to be done by pencil, because this instrument of writing reveals less about the pen lifts, pen pause etc. as in the case of pens.

Fountain Pen:

Fountain pens are used from the ancient time and are considered very classic, very few people are used to its use and thus this is in itself a peculiar feature of its use. The fountain pens generally have two flexible nibs which help in the production of lines of varying width depending mainly on the flexibility of points and pressure applied during writing. Most of the fountain pens of modern scenario have comparatively stiff nib point which restrict shading and produce strokes comparable to the uniform strokes of porous tip pens. One of the most important features of the fountain pens is that they use liquid ink which has a tendency to penetrate deep into the paper fibers. ϖ The fountain pen which consists of broader nib point gives rise to comparatively more shaded strokes and the nature of shading depends on angle of pens.

Requirement:

Pencil, ball pen, porous tip pen, crayon, fountain pen, roller pen, magnifying glass etc.

Procedure:

- Please prepare writing samples using a variety of writing instruments.
- The samples are distributed and the characteristics of the writing material present on the sample document are analyzed.
- Characteristics to consider include thickness of the writing material, strokes, ink absorption on paper, skipping, smudging, etc. and should record their observations in a table. Additionally, the type of writing instrument used to create the sample document can be identified and write down the type of writing instrument they believe was used.
- This exercise will help students develop their observational and analytical skills when it comes to different writing materials and instruments. It will also encourage them to pay attention to details and improve their understanding of the nuances of writing.

Observation Table:

Sample	Characteristic found	Type of writing instrument
1	Stroke? Skipping? Gooping? etc.	Ball pen, pencil, crayon etc.?
2		
3		
4		
5		

Result:

The writing instruments such as ballpoint pens, fountain pens etc., are identified as

a.

b.

c.

d.

e.

Viva Questions:

1. What is the primary characteristic of ballpoint pen ink under a microscope?
2. How can gel pen ink be distinguished from ballpoint pen ink?.
3. What feature distinguishes fountain pen ink in forensic analysis?
4. Which writing instrument typically leaves indentations on the paper surface?
5. What is the main difference between pencil and pen markings under a microscope?
6. How does erasable pen ink behave differently from regular pen ink under UV light?
7. Which writing instrument is most likely to show signs of smudging on a document?
8. What characteristic is unique to felt-tip markers in forensic analysis?
9. How can inkjet printer ink be differentiated from handwritten ink?
10. Which writing instrument's ink can be erased with a standard eraser?

Case Studies:

13

Understanding Paper Manufacturing

Aim:

To understand the paper manufacturing process.

Theory:

Paper is a widely used writing surface, with its origins dating back to the bark of the papyrus plant. The oldest known piece of paper, dating back to around 3500 B.C., can be found in a museum in France. One of the most significant advancements in the paper industry occurred when paper began to be produced from the cellulose content of plants. This breakthrough occurred after 105 A.C. when Ts` ai Lun discovered the process in China. By utilizing old paper cuttings, cannabis fibers, and mineral fibers, Ts` ai Lun was able to create paper.

Manufacturing process of Paper:

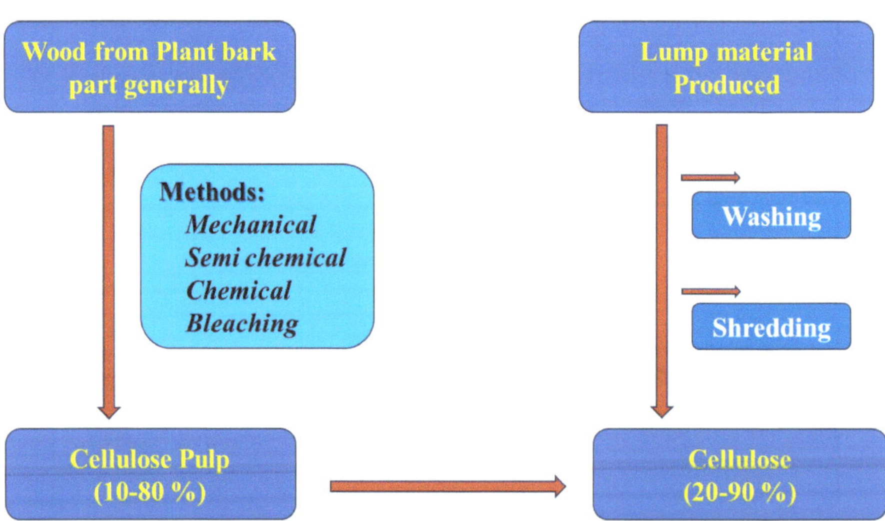

Mechanical beating of the wood to form the lump material. Sizing agents are also added which provide cellular strength to the paper. Some of the sizing agents are as follows:

- *Rosin*
- *Starch*
- *Animal gelatin*
- *Aluminium hydroxide*
- *Synthetic polymers. Loading agents are also used in the manufacturing of paper for providing proper weight to the paper according to the requirement.*
- *Aluminium silicate like kaolin*
- *Magnesium silicate like talcum*
- *Calcium sulphate (Gypsum)*
- *Calcium carbonate.*

After all these steps which have been mentioned above are completed then the sheet formation is done after which a proper coating is given to the paper. This is the last step in paper manufacturing and produces the end product known as paper. Cellulose is used as the raw material for the preparation of paper. The list of some plants with their cellulose content is given below:

S.no.	Name of the Plant	Content of cellulose present
1.	Cotton	92-97%
2.	Hemp	80%
3.	Ramie	85%
4.	Sisal	77%
5.	Common wood	58-67%
6.	Cereal straws	36-37%

Paper is prepared from the wood pulp by mechanical and chemical methods. Newspaper is prepared from the mechanical method while some other writing surfaces used for the purpose of writing is made by chemical process. The composition of paper is decided as the requirement of the work.

Result:

Understanding how paper is made is essential for analyzing and identifying various characteristics of documents. The paper manufacturing process, a crucial aspect of studying questioned document analysis in the lab has been studied and documented.

Viva Questions:

1. What are the primary raw materials used in the paper manufacturing process?
2. Can you explain the basic steps involved in the paper manufacturing process?
3. What is the purpose of the pulping process in paper manufacturing?
4. What are the differences between chemical and mechanical pulping?
5. How does the Kraft process differ from other chemical pulping methods?
6. What role does refining play in the quality of the paper?
7. How is the paper sheet formed in the manufacturing process?
8. Why is consistency in the fiber suspension important during the forming stage?
9. What is the purpose of the pressing stage in paper manufacturing?
10. How is moisture removed from the paper during the drying process?
11. What impact does the drying process have on the final paper properties?
12. What types of finishes can be applied to paper during the finishing process?
13. How does coating improve the properties of paper?
14. What are the environmental impacts of paper manufacturing, and how can they be mitigated?
15. How is water used and recycled in the paper manufacturing process?

Case Studies:

14

Decoding Secret Writing

Aim:

To decode the various types of secret writing.

Theory:

Invisible inks are used for secret writing. These are fluids used to write hidden messages that do not appear unless exposed by a revealing process. Invisible inks can be classified into three main categories:

- those that are revealed by heat,
- those revealed by chemical reactions and
- those that are visible under ultraviolet light

Some common household invisible inks are diluted fruit juices, vinegar and laundry detergent, all which can be applied by a paintbrush, special invisible ink pen or even a toothpick, Historically, used in times of war by governments and insurgents alike. The chemical processes of invisible inks are well known, so a variety of detection methods exist.

Heat-Activated Invisible Inks: Messages written with orange or lime or onion juice can be conveyed by heating the document. Certain salts or organic compounds can also be examined using the same technique.

Inks Developed by Chemical Reactions: Most of them work using pH indicators, so when it doubts, paint or spray a suspected message with a base (like sodium carbonate solution) or an acid (like lemon juice). Some of these inks will reveal their message when heated with vinegar. E.g., i. Phenolphthalein (Ph Indicator), Developed by Ammonia Fumes or Sodium Carbonate (Or another Base), ii. Thymolphthalein, Developed by Ammonia Fumes or Sodium Carbonate (Or Another Base), iii. Vinegar Or Dilute Acetic Acid, Developed by Red Cabbage Water etc.

Ink developed by UV light: Secret writings made using body fluids can be deciphered under UV light. The differential absorption and reflection of

UV rays will help in reading the secret message. Some chemicals also give fluorescence under UV light.

Material Requirements:

Blank papers, cotton buds/ toothpick, burner, UV cabinet, milk, saliva, lemon juice, detergent etc.

Procedure:

Firstly, prepare an invisible ink using vegetable juice or milk or biological fluid or any different chemicals of your choice. Take a cotton bud/toothpick and dipped it in an invisible ink. Apply the invisible ink onto a blank paper (Write any word of your choice). Wait till it completely dry (will invisible to naked eye). Then held the paper to a moderate heat source like burner (heat treatment) or placed the paper in UV cabinet for UV treatment or use ammonia fumes, iodine solution and silver nitrate solution for the development of invisible ink. Observe and note the restored secret writing.

Observation table:

S.No	Sample	Ink Used for Secret Writing	Developer Used for Visualization	Restore (Yes / No)
1.		Milk	Heat	Yes
2.		Lemon Juice	Heat or iodine solution	Yes
3.		Phenolphthalein	Ammonia fumes	Yes
4.		Sodium chloride	Silver nitrate	Yes
5.		Starch	Iodine solution	Yes

Result:

Invisible writing was deciphered successfully using heat, ammonia fumes, iodine solution and silver nitrate solution.

Conclusion:

Secret writing written with different biological, vegetable and chemical fluids and samples deciphered successfully by heat treatment and UV methods.

Forensic Significance:

Generally secret writing is used by Prisoners, Criminals, Terrorists, International spies, Intelligence department, Drug dealers. So, criminal cases these secret writing can be used as potential evidence to arrest a criminal, to prove or disprove the matter under consideration, also helps in linking the crime scene, suspect and criminal.

Viva Questions:

1. What is secret writing?
2. Where do we use secret writing?
3. What is the principle behind the visualization of invisible ink (milk) by using heat?
4. What is the principle behind the visualization of invisible ink (phenolphthalein) by using ammonia fumes?
5. What is the principle behind the visualization of invisible ink (starch) by using iodine solution?
6. What is secret writing, and how is it typically used in questioned documents?
7. Can you describe some common methods used to create secret writing?
8. How can invisible ink be detected on a questioned document?
9. What are some examples of substances commonly used as invisible ink?

10. How does the application of heat help in revealing secret writing?
11. What is micro-writing, and how can it be identified in a forensic examination?
12. What role does chromatography play in the detection of secret writing?
13. How can the use of chemical reagents assist in revealing secret writing on a document?
14. What challenges might arise during the forensic examination of documents with secret writing?
15. Why is it important to consider the possibility of secret writing in forensic document examination?

Case Studies:

15

Stabilization of Charred Document

Aim:

To stabilize the charred documents

Theory:

Charred and torn documents play a crucial role in various cases, often serving as key pieces of evidence. Instances of deliberately charred documents have been documented, where arson was used as a means to destroy important information. Perpetrators often resort to burning documents as a quick and effective method of eliminating incriminating evidence. It is important to note that a charred document does not necessarily mean it has been completely burned, but rather partially damaged by fire. These partially burned documents, known as charred documents, can be restored to a readable state with the appropriate expertise and methods. The characteristics of charred documents include their partially burned state, which can be reversed to make the text legible once again. Understanding the nature of charred documents is essential in forensic investigations and legal proceedings.

- The documents become black due to heat.
- The edges of the documents become curled.
- The document becomes fragile.

Due to the fragility developed the document may break into pieces even by a small amount of pressure.

The charred document always has a point during its burning period at which the written material is clearly seen and at that time the photograph of the document should be taken if possible. Charred documents are more difficult to restore than the torn documents because there is very much difficulty in the process of collecting and transporting the charred documents. The charred document is in very bad condition but still it can be restored the charred document is shown below:

Requirements:

PVA, mesh, tweezers, corrugated box etc.

Procedure:

Protection and transportation of the charred documents:

Charred documents should be picked with great care by putting a hard paper underneath the charred documents. Since the charred documents are fragile and light waited so, at the time of lifting it should be protected from the air. For transportation, it is placed in a special kind of cardboard box known as the corrugated box in which there are layers of cotton and tissue paper on which the charred document is placed. The charred documents should be put very carefully in the corrugated box without any breakage. The topmost layer of this corrugated box consists of cotton so that the document does not break during transportation. The corrugated box should be labeled and sealed with all the necessary details given below:

- Date and time of evidence collection.
- Place of evidence collection.
- Signature of IO and two witnesses.
- Number of evidence in one box etc.

Stabilization of Charred Documents:

- The main problem in the deciphering of the charred document is its fragility. It is that much fragile that it cannot be handled with the hands. So, the first step in deciphering of the charred document is to make it stable for reading or deciphering the matter on the documents.

- There are number of ways which have been in use for the stabilization of the charred documents. One of them is placing the charred documents in the wet moisture chamber for several hours and the spraying of the plasticizers for stabilization.
- The plasticizers used can be cellulose acetate solution in acetone or some other like the polyvinyl acetate (PVA) solution in acetone. But there are various pros and cons to every plasticizer material used.
- The cellulose acetate is a good plasticizer but it cannot be used as regular material here since it cannot be sprayed well which is one of the main characteristics of the stabilizing agents. Gum acacia is another material which can be used for the purpose of stabilization of the charred document but it has a bad property of sticking the glass on which the charred document is placed with the charred document. Moreover the spraying property of the gum acacia is also not good.
- The third and most preferable is the polyvinyl acetate either it can be sprayed or applied with the help of a glass rod to whole of the paper with constant pressure and uniformity. Before the application of polyvinyl acetate the glass surface should be polished with 1% solution of silicon type water repellant substance in petroleum-ether.
- Due to this silicon type water repellant substance the charred document does not get bound to the glass on application of the polyvinyl acetate.
- Thus, the document can be lifted with ease after being stabilized by stabilizing agent. The polyvinyl acetate solution is made in acetone which gets evaporated after application.
- After this step the stretching power of the paper is gained to some extent and thus it can be preserved for deciphering the content of the document either between two Perspex sheets or between two glass pieces.

Result:

The preservation and stabilization of charred documents have been learned and documented.

Viva Questions:

1. What is a charred document, and why is it important in forensic investigations?
2. What are the primary challenges in handling and analyzing charred documents?
3. What precautions should be taken when collecting charred documents from a crime scene?
4. Why is it essential to document the condition of a charred document before attempting any preservation techniques?
5. What role does humidity control play in the preservation of charred documents?
6. How can charred documents be stabilized before further examination?
7. What is the purpose of using consolidants in the preservation of charred documents?
8. How should a charred document be stored once it has been stabilized?
9. What techniques are used to enhance the readability of charred documents?
10. How can chemical treatments assist in the stabilization and analysis of charred documents?
11. What is the significance of digital imaging in the analysis of charred documents?
12. Why is it important to avoid direct exposure to light during the analysis of charred documents?
13. What challenges arise when attempting to separate pages of a charred document?

14. How can forensic examiners ensure that the stabilization process does not alter the original document content?
15. What legal and ethical considerations must be taken into account when preserving and stabilizing charred documents?

Case Studies:

Sources and References

1. https://www.researchgate.net/publication/358907393_General_Characteristics_of_Handwriting_and_its_Psychological_Importance/link/622210ab97401151d2fbf85c/download?_tp=eyJjb250ZXh0Ijp7ImZpcnN0UGFnZSI6InB1YmxpY2F0aW9uIiwicGFnZSI6InB1YmxpY2F0aW9uIn19
2. https://www.researchgate.net/publication/338576972_Graphology_based_Handwritten_Character_Analysis_for_Human_Behavior_Identification
3. https://www.pinterest.com/pin/pseudoscience-graphology--301882599816786800/
4. https://www.fountainpennetwork.com/forum/topic/372710-if-you-like-good-handwriting-dont-look-at-this-a-requested-handwriting-sample/
5. https://epgp.inflibnet.ac.in/epgpdata/uploads/epgp_content/S001608/P001743/M027861/ET/1521090883m22-etext.pdf
6. https://www.businesstechweekly.com/productivity/document-imaging/laser-printer-inkjet/
7. https://epgp.inflibnet.ac.in/epgpdata/uploads/epgp_content/S000016FS/P000695/M011493/ET/1516193591FSC_P8_M9_e-text.pdf
8. https://www.reddit.com/r/chemistry/comments/h8ig8r/pen_ink_tlc_i_did_in_orgo_1_lab_we_tested_4/?rdt=41535
9. https://epgp.inflibnet.ac.in/epgpdata/uploads/epgp_content/S000016FS/P000695/M006287/ET/1516193543FSC_P8_M7_e-text.pdf
10. https://epgp.inflibnet.ac.in/Home/ViewSubject?catid=eCJfy23Kjy3c0vICLa6VYg==

Biography of Miss Labhini Rahangdale

Miss. Labhini Rahangdale holds a Master of Science degree in Forensic Science and is currently an Assistant Professor, specializing in forensic fingerprint and questioned document analysis. With two years of teaching experience, Miss. Labhini Rahangdale has effectively imparted knowledge in various forensic subjects, ensuring that students gain a comprehensive understanding of the field. Miss. Labhini Rahangdale has also qualified the University Grants Commission National Eligibility Test (UGC NET). Before transitioning to academia, Miss. Labhini Rahangdale served as a Senior Forensic Analyst in a private company. In this role, Miss. Labhini Rahangdale was responsible for handling a variety of fire and arson-related cases, applying rigorous scientific methods and critical thinking to solve complex forensic challenges. Miss. Labhini Rahangdale has knowledge in fingerprint and questioned document analysis, combined with practical experience in the field, makes a valuable contributor to both the academic and professional forensic communities.

Biography of Dr. Raju Nandhakumar

Dr. R. Nandhakumar, a professor, specializes in organic and supramolecular chemistry. He received both his UG, PG and Ph.D., degree in Chemistry from Bharathiar University, Coimbatore, Tamil Nadu, India. Presently, he is the Professor of Chemistry at the Division of Physical Sciences, Karunya Institute of Technology and Science. His research interests include Carbon-based materials, Fluorescent Chemosensors, and Forensic Science. He has successfully completed several projects from various funding agencies and guided six doctoral students. To his credit, he has written four books, seven book chapters, two international patents (granted), fifteen national patents (twelve granted), and published more than 190 research papers (including five review articles) in peer-reviewed international and national journals.

www.ingramcontent.com/pod-product-compliance
Ingram Content Group UK Ltd.
Pitfield, Milton Keynes, MK11 3LW, UK
UKHW061027310726
14090UKWH00024B/445

* 9 7 9 8 8 9 5 8 8 4 3 8 6 *